60
BULLETIN BOARD IDEAS

TO TEACH AND INSPIRE

BY CAROLINE BOENDER

ILLUSTRATED BY BOB BURCHETT

STANDARD
PUBLISHING
Cincinnati, Ohio

DEDICATION

To Mom and Dad:

Your example of quiet faith has taught me to trust in God,

Your patience has allowed me time to grow and develop the talents which God has given me,

Your encouragement has gently prodded me to do my best, and to persevere even through difficult tasks,

Your love has shown me how to love others in return.

Caroline

Scripture quotations are from the HOLY BIBLE— NEW INTERNATIONAL VERSION, Copyright ©1973, 1978, 1984 International Bible Society. Used by permission of Zondervan Bible Publishers. All rights reserved.

The "NIV" and "New International Version" trademarks are registered in the United States Patent and Trademark Office by International Bible Society. Use of either trademark requires the permission of International Bible Society.

The Standard Publishing Company, Cincinnati, Ohio
A division of Standex International Corporation

00 99 98 97 96 95 94 93   5 4 3 2 1

Library of Congress Cataloging-in-Publication Data

Boender, Caroline.
    60 bulletin board ideas : to teach and inspire /by Caroline Boender.
        p.   cm.
    Includes indexes.
    ISBN 0-87403-869-3
    1. Christian education--Bulletin boards. 2. Bible --Study and
teaching.   I. Title.   II. Title: Sixty bulletin board ideas.
BV1535.25.B64   1993
268' .635--dc20
                                                92-18675
                                                CIP

CONTENTS

Use this bulletin board when teaching about Noah and the flood, or when assigning Genesis 8:22 as a memory selection. This bulletin board can also be used as part of a unit on God's promises and His care for us.

Background: light blue
Border: none
Caption: black
Rainbow: from top to bottom - red, orange, yellow, green, blue, purple
Dove: white
Altar: pieces of gray paper overlapping each other, with black shading

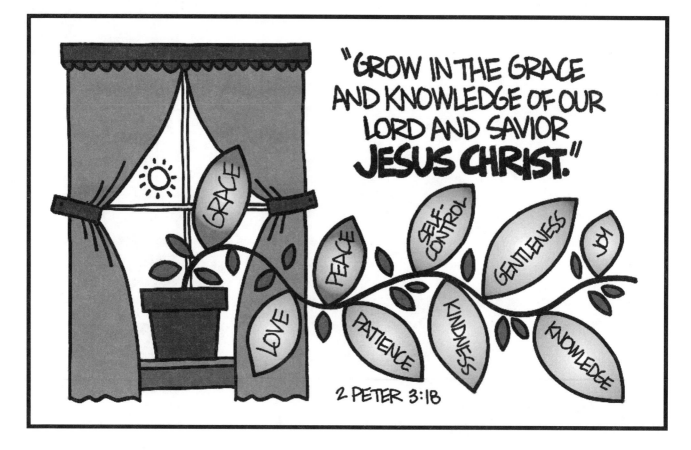

Use this bulletin board at the beginning of a church or school year to challenge church members and students to grow as Christians. This bulletin board could also be used to promote a Bible study, especially one about the fruit of the Spirit.

Variation for lower-elementary grade classrooms: On each leaf, write a reference for a Bible verse that your students will be memorizing.

Background:	orange, or possibly large sheet of scrap wallpaper
Border:	light blue
Caption:	light blue
Curtains:	bright fabric pleated and tacked at the top; pulled to the sides with strips of fabric or trim
Flower Pot:	brick red
Vine:	green rug yarn or paper
Leaves:	green
Window Sill:	brown paper or wood grain wall paper
Window View:	light blue

IN THE BEGINNING

GOD CREATED THE HEAVENS AND THE EARTH

GENESIS 1:1

Background: royal blue—use corrugated cardboard, gift wrap, construction paper, or burlap

Border: bright red

Caption: trace each word on yellow paper, using one-inch letter patterns. Leave a lot of space between words. Then cut around each word.

Pictures: have your students collect pictures of things God has made. These pictures should be large enough to see from a distance. If you wish, you and your students can mount the pictures on colored construction paper.

Turn this bulletin board into a hands-on learning center by asking the children to bring things God has made, such as leaves or acorns. Display these objects on a table located near the bulletin board so that the children can look at, touch, smell, and even listen to each other's objects.

THE EARTH IS THE LORD'S, AND EVERYTHING IN IT...
PSALM 24:1 (NIV)

Use this bulletin board during a study of creation. Involve young children by asking them to make the apples, flowers, and rabbits. This bulletin board would also be appropriate for Earth Day. Individual classes could plan and implement ways to care for the world God has made.

Background:	white or a neutral tone
Circle:	light blue
Mat:	green
Caption:	orange or yellow foil gift wrap or paper
Tree:	brown and green
Apples:	red foil gift wrap
Rabbit:	white quilt batting
Clouds:	white quilt batting
Grass:	green fringed paper
Flowers:	assorted
Bush:	green with blue berries

Use this bulletin board to record arrivals of babies throughout the year, or as part of your church's cradle roll program.

Background: small print fabric in pastel colors

Caption: complementary pastel color. An alternate caption could be "Beary" Precious Bundles.

Quilt: done in a variety of pastel colors. Use paper with names and dates of births written in calligraphy. Or use an actual quilt on which names and dates are embroidered, and later display the quilt in your church's nursery.

Bears: light brown

Bow: red

9

Use this bulletin board to record new births and adoptions. You might want to use actual gift-wrapped boxes attached to the bulletin board to give it a three-dimensional effect.

Background:	light green gingham fabric or paper
Caption:	yellow
Border:	yellow
Packages:	pastel colored gift wrap or construction paper, with names and dates of birth of children. Add bows made from actual ribbon.

Background: blue gingham fabric, gift wrap, or paper

Border: yellow

Caption: yellow and orange paper slightly overlapping each other for a three dimensional effect

Raindrops: white, outlined in black, with words written in various colored markers

Umbrella: painted with assorted colors of tempera paint, such as pink, purple, aqua, lime, and orange.

On each raindrop, write a way God shows His love to us, such as through family, friends, pets, beauty in nature, homes, His Word, clothes, and other blessings.

Display this bulletin board when teaching about the four seasons of God's creation. If you teach very young children, find several pictures depicting each season. Ask your students to help you decide which season each picture depicts. Place each picture on the board by the section of the tree that represents that season. As an accompanying activity, memorize Genesis 6:22.

Variation: Discuss the various ways in which God demonstrates His providential love to us throughout the year. Add details to sections of the tree. To represent winter, sponge paint white tempera on the branches. Add tiny silk flower blossoms (from silk flower arrangements) to depict spring.

Background:	light blue
Border:	yellow
Caption:	yellow or assorted colors
Tree Trunk:	brown
Spring Tree:	leaves are smaller and light green; blossoms pink and white tissue
Fall Tree:	leaves are various fall colors
Summer Tree:	leaves are green
Winter Tree:	bare branches of tree

This bulletin board can serve as a simple but poignant reminder of God's love for us. Display this either near the entrance of your church or in your classroom. If your church provides counseling services, use this bulletin board to promote that ministry.

Background: blue gingham fabric or construction paper

Border: orange

Grass: green paper cut with slits

Caption: orange

Daisies: green stems and leaves; white petals; yellow center

Sun: yellow

Display this bulletin board when teaching a lesson on God's mercy and grace in our lives. If your class or Bible study likes to sing, sing "Great Is Thy Faithfulness" or "When Morning Gilds the Sky" to reinforce the theme.

Alternative use: Display this bulletin board in your church foyer to remind your entire congregation of God's goodness.

Background:	tissue gift wrap, in shades of purple, blue, and pink
Border:	none
Caption:	black in sky background, white on mountain background
Sun:	yellow
Sun's Rays:	shades of orange and red
Mountains:	purple or black

The bare trees are evidence of the barrenness of winter, and symbolize the unfruitful, lonely, and difficult times in our lives. Display this bulletin board in a prominent place as a reminder for us to trust God in all seasons of our lives.

Snow:	white
Sky:	light blue
Caption:	dark blue or purple
Trees:	green with pulled out cotton along branches
Bird:	red cardinal

Many families chose to vacation in August. Display pictures of scenic places to visit, as well as pictures of activities that can be done right at home. Display this bulletin board in the summer when many church members are on vacation. Add pictures of local, state, and national attractions. This bulletin board can also be used at the end of a school year. Display pictures of activities in which students plan to participate during the summer, as well as places which they will visit.

Background: yellow
Border: red, orange, or blue
Caption: same as the border
Car: red, orange, or blue (different than the border and caption)
Road: black

Background: blue, yellow, orange, or green gingham fabric

Border: orange, red, or blue

Caption: assorted colors

Railroad track: black yarn or paper

Train Cars: assorted colors

Puffs of smoke: white cotton balls

On the train cars, write names of Bible people. List descriptions of those characters on rectangular pieces of paper (assorted colors or white). Have students match the person with the correct description by tucking the rectangles into the correct train car. To make this bulletin board self-correcting write the answers on the backs of the rectangles. If you wish, add trees and other scenery to the background.

Write questions about the Bible or a Bible story on the top part of the question mark. On the bottom (dot) parts, write the answers. Paper punch a hole in each answer dot so students can hang it under the correct question mark.

Background:	natural burlap, or a gingham fabric
Border:	red
Caption:	red
Question Marks:	top part: assorted colors; bottom parts: white
Boy:	draw person on white paper and color with markers

CHRISTMAS ★ QUESTIONS

Background: yellow
Border: red, green, or purchased Christmas print or gift wrap
Caption: red
Tree: green
Star: gold foil gift wrap or yellow paper
Ornaments: assorted bright color

On each ornament write a question related to the prophecy of Christ's coming, or Christmas. On the inside of each folded ornament, write the correct answer. Staple the ornaments onto the bulletin board so that the answers are hidden, but can be uncovered easily.

On the front side of each apple, write a question about creation. On the back write the answer. Paper punch a hole near the top of each apple so students can hang the apples on the tree as they correctly answer the questions.

Background:	blue gingham fabric
Border:	red
Grass:	green
Caption:	yellow or orange
Flowers:	assorted colors
Butterflies:	assorted colors
Tree:	brown trunk; green leaves; red apples

On each fish write a true or untrue statement about Jesus and His disciples. On the back of each fish, write whether or not the statement is a fact. Paper punch a hole in each fish so students can place them on the bulletin board.

Background:	blue gingham fabric
Border:	red
Caption:	red
Fish:	assorted colors
Fishing line:	brown
Hook:	grey
Worm:	brown

Write questions about biblical accounts on the rabbits, and write the correct answers on the tails. Paper punch a hole near the top of each tail so students can place the tail on the correct rabbit.

Background:	red or royal blue burlap, gingham fabric, or paper
Border:	yellow
Caption:	yellow
Rabbits:	assorted shades of brown, grey, white, and black
Tails:	white
Tufts of Grass:	small rectangles of green paper with slits cut one-half inch apart from each other and curled to resemble grass

Write names of Bible characters on the bowls. Write four or five descriptions of each characters on pieces of popcorn-shaped paper. Ask your students to match the descriptions of Bible character with their names by placing the popcorn in the correct bowls. After students have mastered the information found on this board, you may wish to treat them to a popcorn party.

Background: natural burlap
Border: red
Caption: red letters on a piece of white paper that has been scalloped to resemble popcorn
Bowls: assorted colors
Popcorn: white

Use this bulletin board to help students learn which books of the Bible are found in the Old Testament, and which are found in the New Testament. Write the names of the books of the Bible on pieces of paper cut to resemble giraffe spots. Have students attach each spot to the correct giraffe. Write the correct answer on the back of each spot so students can check their work. You may wish to add branches and leaves cut from paper to the upper left and right corners to give the bulletin board a jungle-like effect.

Background: blue
Border: green
Caption: green
Giraffe: yellow
Spots: orange

Background: blue, yellow, or green gingham fabric

Border: purchased border with a bear print, or red paper

Caption: assorted colors

Bears: brown, white, and tan

T-shirts: assorted bright colors. Punch a hole in each shoulder so that the T-shirts can be hung on straight pins.

Use this bulletin board to help your students learn to match Bible characters and events. Ask students to match each T-shirt with the correct bear.

Variation: Use this board to match other biblical facts such as Bible parents to their children or Bible verses to their references.

Each student makes a lily pad for each verse to be learned during the unit or quarter. On the lily pads, write the references for the memory verses. Make a frog for each student, and write each student's name on it. As a student learns a verse, have the pupil move his or her frog forward to the next lily pad.

Background:	light blue
Border:	pink, yellow, or orange
Caption:	pink, yellow, or orange
Frogs:	dark green
Lily Pads:	light green

On each balloon, draw a stripe for each verse to be learned during the unit or quarter. Color a section of the balloon each time a Bible verse is memorized.

Background:	blue gingham fabric or paper
Border:	rainbow striped (purchased), or red or orange paper
Caption:	assorted bright colors
Clouds:	white quilt batting or paper
Balloons:	white paper or poster board
Baskets:	brown, with a student's name written on each basket

Write out the verses to be memorized for the month or quarter, and attach them to the bulletin board, along with the squirrel.

Variation: Make a squirrel for each student. As each student memorizes a verse have him or her place an acorn with the Scripture reference written on it near his or her squirrel.

Background:	orange or yellow burlap, gingham fabric, dotted fabric, or gift wrap
Border:	fall print (purchased), brown construction paper, or overlapping leaves cut from assorted fall colors of paper
Caption:	brown
Squirrel:	brown paper or purchased
Acorns:	shades of brown and olive green
Tree Trunk:	brown; exposed surface should be tan or lighter brown

Background: natural or white burlap, or white paper
Border: green
Caption: green
Grapes: purple, with green leaves

Copy the pattern onto purple paper. The number of grapes should equal the number of Scripture verses to be memorized. Use green for the leaves. Attach each bunch of grapes to board with a name of a student written on each leaf. As a student memorizes a Scripture, he could record the reference on a grape in his bunch.

Add pictures from real seed packets or seed catalogs to give the bulletin board theme more authenticity.

Background:	blue or green gingham fabric
Border:	orange
Caption:	orange
Flowers:	assorted bright colors
Seed packets:	assorted bright colors

Encourage students, Bible study members, and your church members to share their faith in the Lord. Together, pray and discuss ways to reach out to people in your community, school, and workplace with the good news of Christ's love. Encourage each other to implement those plans.

Background:	natural burlap or a bright color of gingham fabric
Border:	orange or red
Caption:	black or brown, except for *FAITH* which should be made of five different colors of bright paper
Letters:	draw eyes, noses, and mouths on the letters of *FAITH.* Use chenille wire to make arms and hands.

This bulletin board is based on Psalm 100. Use this bulletin board to teach about praise and worship. Incorporate a study of Psalm 100 in your Sunday school classes or weekly Bible studies. Work with your pastor to plan a worship service in which your students can also participate. You may also wish to display this bulletin board near the entrance of your church sanctuary.

Background:	blue or green gingham fabric or paper
Border:	orange, red, or purple
Caption:	assorted bright colors
Church:	white or light brown, with multi-colored windows to resemble stained glass
Music Notes:	assorted colors

Background: multi-colored streaked tissue gift wrap paper or light blue paper

Border: none

Caption: black

Sun: orange

Praise: rainbow effect
P - purple
R - blue
A - green
I - yellow
S - orange
E - red

This bulletin board idea can be used for a month of emphasis on music or worship. Contact the person who coordinates the worship service to have a congregational reading of Psalm 50.

With your students, discuss how we as Christians can glorify and praise God in all areas of our lives. Look for answers like eating, playing, working, or sleeping.

Alternate border: Cut shapes of people from assorted colors of paper, and overlap to form a border.

Background:	blue, yellow, or green gingham fabric or paper, or natural burlap
Border:	orange, blue, or red
Caption:	assorted colors of construction paper
Pictures:	choose pictures of children in a variety of activities, settings, and ethnic backgrounds. Mount pictures on paper that is the same color as the caption.

Background: royal blue burlap or construction paper
Border: red
Caption: silver glitter applied to white letters; red foil gift wrap; or red construction paper
Rocket: cut a rocket from a large piece of cardboard or poster board. Cover it with aluminum foil.

Use this bulletin board to publicize Vacation Bible School. Add posters containing information about the time and location of Vacation Bible School. Change the number on the rocket each day (or week). This bulletin board can also be used to announce the coming of other church activities not held all year long, such as a boy's or girl's club.

Write the names of the children in your Sunday School. Add new flowers as additional children begin to attend. You may wish to write information about your Sunday School activities on a large flower. This bulletin board can also be used to promote other activities such as Vacation Bible School.

Background:	blue or yellow gingham fabric
Border:	a bright color that complements the background fabric
Caption:	same as border
Flowers:	stems: chenille wire; leaves: green; petals: assorted colors

Attach information about your church's Vacation Bible School. This bulletin board can also be used to promote other activities for children, such as Sunday School.

Background:	blue gingham fabric, burlap, or construction paper
Border:	pink
Caption:	pink
Rabbits:	white

Does your church promote fellowship by planning church family events such as bowling, skating, and potluck dinners? Promote these events via this bulletin board.

Background: light green
Border: none
Caption: black
Silhouettes: various colors

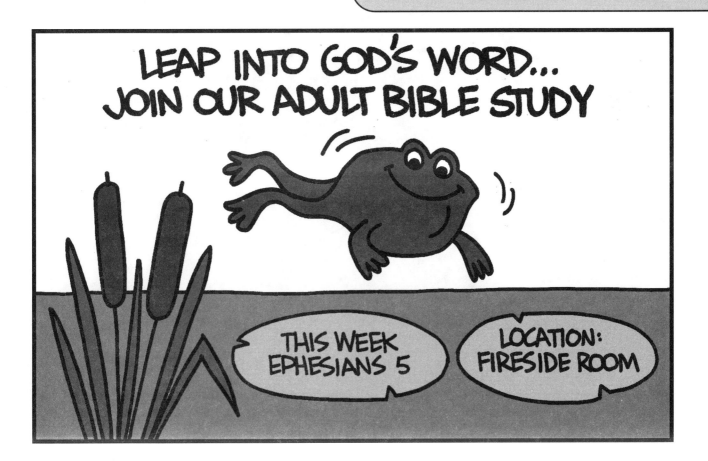

Use this bulletin board to promote a Bible study, a film series, or an all-church Bible memorization project.

Background:	light blue
Border:	yellow
Caption:	yellow
Frog:	dark green
Lily Pads:	light green
Lilies:	pink
Cattails:	brown

Promote various activities and organizations of your church with this bulletin board. In addition to naming the groups, you may wish to include the time and location of each group's meeting, as well.

Background: blue gingham fabric
Caption: red
Border: red
Cookies: white or pale yellow
Cookie Jar: red or bright yellow

Attach information about upcoming concerts on the bottom right side of the bulletin board. Include date, time, and if possible, a picture of the person or persons performing.

Background:	foil gift wrap or construction paper, in a color appropriate for the season
Border:	none
Caption and notes:	black
Keyboard:	black and white

Attach book jackets to this bulletin board. Or involve the children in your church by asking them to design book jackets or posters of their favorite books from the church library.

Background: blue or green gingham fabric or construction paper
Border: orange
Caption: orange
Goat: white or grey
Grass: green

Use this bulletin board to promote Vacation Bible School. Cut out large shapes in various bright colors. On each shape write a name of an activity for VBS. Cut out shapes for a wheelbarrow. Place shapes in it.

Variation: You can use this bulletin board to promote any other children's activity.

Background:	yellow burlap or construction paper
Border:	orange
Caption:	orange
Wheelbarrow:	red
Wheelbarrow Contents:	assorted bright colors
Wheel:	black
Handles:	brown

Display this bulletin board in your classroom. Print your students' names on the small sheep. You may even wish to have each student make his/her own sheep.

Note: You will need to explain the meaning of "ewe" to young children.

Background:	natural burlap or light green gingham fabric or paper
Border:	yellow or orange
Caption:	yellow or orange
Large Sheep:	make this from white, light-weight cardboard, covered with cotton balls
Small Sheep:	white paper, with students' names written on them

Background: blue gingham fabric
Border: pink
Caption: pink
Large Bear: use a light brown sewn and stuffed bear, if available
Small Bears: assorted shades of brown, with students names written on them

Place this bulletin board in a spot where it will be seen immediately by students entering your classroom.

Variation: Display this bulletin board in a central location during your Vacation Bible School week. As new students arrive each day, write each child's name on a bear before adding it to the bulletin board.

Use this board to encourage people of all ages to serve God throughout the year by serving others. Discuss with your students ways in which they can spread joy to others, and then help them complete a project of service.

Background: blue
Border: none
Caption: red except for "JOY" which should be yellow
People: silhouettes of red, yellow, brown, black, and white

Background: natural burlap
Border: assorted colors
Caption: assorted colors
Heart: collage on large piece of lightweight cardboard

Use natural colored burlap for the background of this bulletin board and a variety of colors for the caption. Cut one large heart from a large piece of construction paper or lightweight cardboard. Have each student find and cut out several pictures of children from magazines. Paste the pictures onto the heart shape, overlapping them so that the background does not show. Each child should write his or her name on a small heart and hang it on the board.

Display a photograph of each of your students on hearts.

Variation: Ask each student to draw a picture of a way Jesus shows His love to us, or a way we can show our love to Him.

Background:	natural colored burlap
Border:	twisted red and white crepe paper streamers
Caption:	red
Hearts:	red

Background: green
Border: yellow
Caption: yellow and orange, overlapping each other slightly

Spring brings an abundance of new life. Ask your students to bring pictures of their own baby animals, as well as pictures of baby brothers, sisters, and cousins.

Variation: Ask your students to cut pictures of baby animals from magazines. To turn this bulletin board into a learning center, place a table nearby. Ask students to look for and bring signs of spring and new life. Discuss the items, and display them on the table.

Use this bulletin board in a unit on praise. You may wish to add pictures of ways that people and all of God's creation show praise to God.

Variation: Ask students to jot down in graffiti-style ways to praise God. Memorize Psalm 113:3.

Background:	lavender
Border:	purple or green
Caption:	purple or green
Cross:	brown with yellow trim
Rays of Light:	yellow

JESUS GIVES NEW LIFE!

Background: pale pink or blue

Border: twisted aqua or purple crepe paper

Caption: aqua (same color as border)

Butterfly: bright pastels (purple, hot pink, aqua) with black features

To give the butterfly a two-dimensional effect, cut bright pastel-colored tissue paper into one-inch squares. Place a square around the eraser end of a pencil, add a dot of glue to the tissue paper, and attach to a piece of lightweight cardboard cut in the shape of a butterfly. Repeat the process until the butterfly is complete. A border could be made using the same process.

Display this bulletin board in a prominent place for your Easter morning church services. You can also use this in your classroom when teaching children about the Easter story.

Background:	light blue
Border:	none
Caption:	white or pink
Sun:	yellow or orange
Sun Rays:	purple cut from two-inch wide strips of construction paper

REMEMBER ME

This bulletin board can serve as a simple but powerful reminder to people of all ages of Christ's sacrificial love. Display this bulletin board during Holy Week, or throughout the entire Lenten season.

Background: gray or blue
Border: black
Caption: black
Grapes: purple
Bread: brown or gold

Display this bulletin board just prior to Ascension Day, and when teaching about Christ's ascension and His second coming.

Optional: On the hill place pictures or silhouettes of people gazing upward.

Background:	blue, purple, and pink streaked gift wrap, or blue, purple, and pink watercolor paint brushed onto white paper
Border:	dark blue
Caption:	dark blue
Hill & Crosses:	purple or black
Clouds:	white
Sun:	yellow and orange

Use this bulletin board idea when your church or Sunday school studies the importance of the Holy Spirit.

Variation: As a class project, research the Bible and find other names and figures that represent the Holy Spirit. List them on the board using smaller letters than the caption.

Background:	blue
Border:	orange
Caption:	orange
Dove:	white
Fire:	orange, red, and yellow

Use this bulletin board to teach students the locations of various scenic places in our country, and to show the variety of God's creation as found in our country. Calendars and magazines contain excellent pictures. To turn this bulletin board into a learning center place a table nearby. Ask students to bring pictures and souvenirs which they have gotten from various places in our country. Discuss them, and display them on the table.

Background:	medium or dark burlap or construction paper
Border:	red
Caption:	red
Map Outline:	white with lettering done with black markers
Pictures:	mount on red construction paper. Connect to correct location map, using red yarn.

Attach pictures of various places in our country, cut from magazines and calendars. To turn this bulletin board into a learning center place a table nearby. Ask students to bring pictures and other items from other countries. For a starter, have students discover where the various everyday items in their homes were made. Discuss the items and pictures, and display them on the table.

Background:	white burlap
Border:	red paper or red, white, and blue crepe paper streamer
Caption:	red foil gift wrap
Flag:	red, white, and blue

Assemble this bulletin board prior to Thanksgiving Day. Students should cut out pictures of things for which your students are thankful. Provide magazines for your students to use as a source of pictures. You may wish to glue the pictures to a large piece of construction paper before attaching them to the bulletin board.

Background: a collage of pictures
Border: orange
Caption: orange

GLORY TO THE NEWBORN KING!

Background:	royal blue burlap or foil gift wrap
Border:	gold metallic Christmas tree garland
Caption:	red or gold foil gift wrap
Star and Crown:	gold foil gift wrap
Crown Jewels:	various bright colors
Manger:	brown or wood grain wallpaper
Hay:	yellow or real straw

Young children will especially enjoy looking at and touching this bulletin board. Make the scene as realistic as possible by using real straw in the manger, adding two-dimensional jewels to the crown, and securely attaching an actual doll to the bulletin board.

A picture of the stable scene can also be added to the bulletin board. Another option would be to display an actual nativity scene on a table near the bulletin board. Use unbreakable figures, so that your students will be free to touch them.

Background:	dark blue or natural burlap
Border:	red and gold foil Christmas tree garland
Starburst Shape:	gold foil gift wrap
Flames:	orange and yellow construction paper
"JOY":	red felt or construction paper
Caption:	red foil gift wrap

Background: gold foil gift wrap or natural burlap

Border: red and gold metallic Christmas tree garland

Caption: red foil gift wrap

Wreath: shapes of hands traced by students, cut from green foil gift wrap or green paper. Overlap the hands to form a wreath

Hearts: red foil

Bow: red velvet ribbon

Christmas is a time when we celebrate God's love as shown by the gift of His Son. As you help your students prepare this bulletin board, you may also list ways to show God's love to others in your area during the Christmas season. As you share God's love with the lonely and less fortunate, your students will experience His love returning full circle to them, as symbolized by the wreath.

MAY THE WARMTH OF CHRIST'S LOVE FILL YOUR HEART THIS SEASON.

Ask church members to attach Christmas cards to the "bricks" to share their Christmas wishes with others in your church family.

Bricks:	red paper with black lines drawn on it to suggest bricks
Interior of Fireplace:	gray
Caption:	gold foil gift wrap
Flames:	orange, gold, and red foil gift wrap or paper
Logs:	brown, gray, or black paper

Background:	yellow
Border:	silver metallic Christmas tree garland
Caption:	black construction paper with silver glitter added to the edges of the letters
Hills:	black construction paper
Nativity Figures:	black construction paper

This bulletin board is striking in its simplicity. Use yellow paper for the background. Add the hills and nativity scene figures, both cut from black construction paper to produce a silhouette effect. Cut the caption from black construction paper, but add silver glitter to the edges of the letters. For a finishing touch, place a silver Christmas tree garland along the sides and at the top of the board. At the bottom part of the bulletin board, include the dates and times of special worship services to be held in your church and community during the Christmas season.

Display an unbreakable nativity scene on a nearby table so that your students can retell the story of Christ's birth. Make costumes available for the students to dress up in, and ask the students to act out the Christmas story during a free time.

Background:	red foil gift wrap or printed gift wrap
Border:	gold metallic garland
Caption:	gold foil gift wrap or green construction paper
Manger:	brown construction paper or add real straw if possible

Ornament Pattern
for idea on page 19

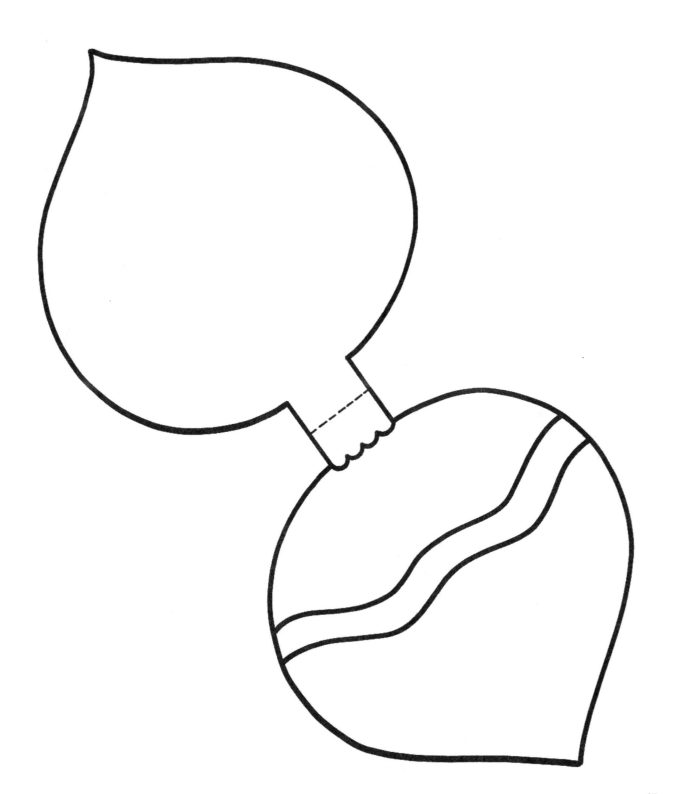

Apple Pattern
for idea on page 20

Rabbit Pattern
for idea on page 22

Bear Pattern
for ideas on pages 25 and 45

Frog Pattern

for idea on page 26

T-Shirt
for idea on page 25

Rabbit Tail Pattern
for idea on page 22

Lily Pad Pattern
for idea on page 26

Balloon Pattern
for idea on page 27

Stained-glass-window
Pattern
for idea on page 32

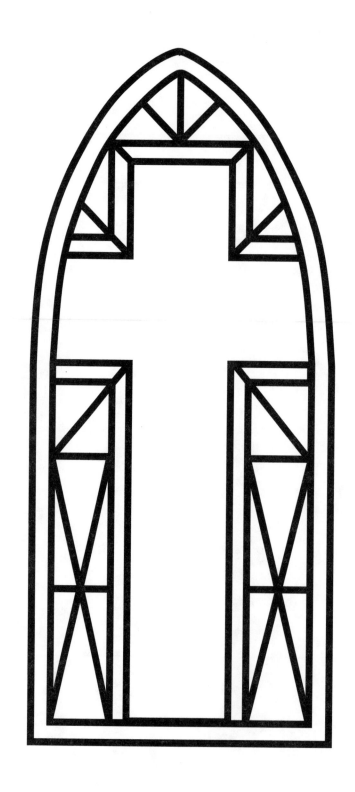

Lonely Man Pattern

for idea on page 39

Dove Pattern

for idea on page 55

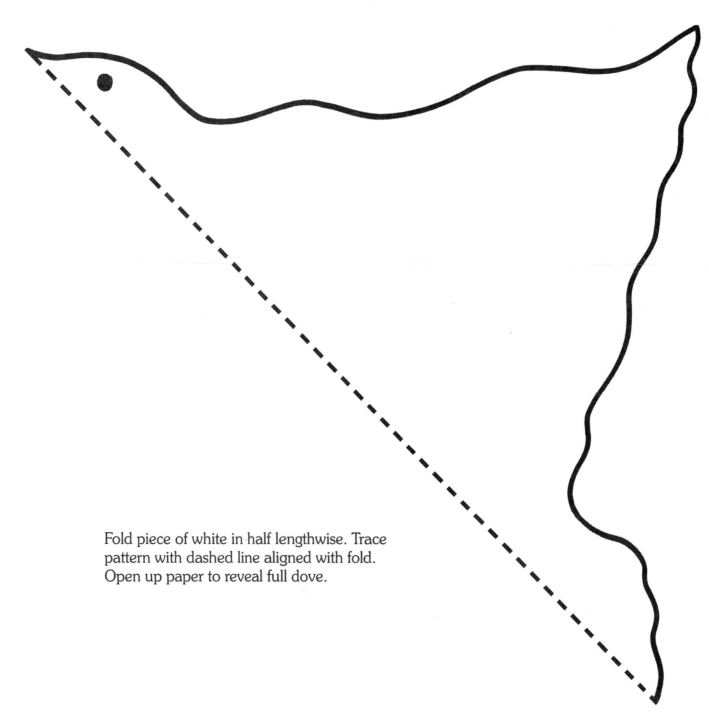

Fold piece of white in half lengthwise. Trace
pattern with dashed line aligned with fold.
Open up paper to reveal full dove.